ODE TO DYMPHNA

Poems by

NINA BELÉN ROBINS

Thompson & Columbus, Inc., Publishers
New York

ISBN: 979-8-9869385-0-9

Cover and Book Design
Mark Wedemeyer / Carbon13 Design Bureau

www.thompsonandcolumbus.com

DEDICATED TO BUSPAR

Be prepared to be shaken and stirred by Nina Robins's brilliant new poetry anthology, *Ode to Dymphna.*

Robins presents us with a host of startling, disconcerting (and sometimes hilarious) connections and juxtapositions. She reveals the inconsolable bitterness that can hide within the gift of pearl earrings or the deep tenderness within the contemplation of a chicken.

In one evolving series of poems, she traces the arc between a child's resentful, bewildering first encounter with the mental health system and the adult's sober gratitude for the pill that finally works.

In another, she takes us from the distress of a social media ghosting to the terrifying thought that a beloved partner might die. She gives us new ways to think about losing weight and deleting e-mails and peeing in the woods. And about the unexpected turns of fate that can lead us back to faith.

— S. W. Leicher, author of the novels
   Acts of Assumption and *Acts of Atonement*

CONTENTS

ODE TO DYMPHNA

PREFACE

Thoughts on faith

ODE TO BACTERIA

Sometimes I wonder if bacteria pray.
Swim along their host
and wonder where they came from.
Thank the body where they live
for the warmth they call home.
Mourn the death of their loved ones
when their time is up,
or when the medicine works,
or when their host dies.
I wonder if the bad bacteria
make war with the good,
if they can tell the difference.
If there are battles for areas of skin,
for food.
If the famine of cleanliness
wipes out entire colonies.
If they wonder where sanitizer comes from.
See immunity as evolution.
Rejoice in tolerance
for antibiotics,
claim death of weaker varieties
as natural selection.
I wonder if bacteria come in race,
have hierarchy,
call the stronger ones leader,
follow them blindly.
Can see outside the body,
know we are aware of their presence,
feel guilty when we medicate
and obliterate them.
Preach that we know which ones we punish,
try to change the ones they blame.
I wonder if they call us God.

Their big world a dot,
a crevice,
a membrane.
We are giant and powerful and almighty.
I wonder if they know we are smaller than so much else.
Fallible.
Just as fragile as they are,
just as mortal.
That we call the space we live on earth,
universe.
That we are born, and die,
and damage,
and fight,
and love,
and prey,
and kill,
and cleanse.
That we are small beings in huge spaces.
That we get wiped out
with famine,
and disease.
That we do not know where we came from.
That we also are so small,
on a bigger being,
in a big space.
I wonder if they know
we pray.

POEMS

The odes and ends

ODE TO RUSTY BOTTLE CAPS

I hate the couch so we sit at the table,
me fitting, she squeezed into a kid's chair.
We play poker with beer bottle caps
I have in an espresso canister
like Bert from Sesame Street,
but his never seem rusty.

In third grade most kids don't play poker.
I know how and here we are in this office
with my stinky bottle caps together for an hour.
Did you have a good day?
Did you play with the other children?
Did you fight with anyone?
Yes. I had a good day.
I don't buy it Nina. You don't have good days.
You're not happy.
She crouches in the chair,
trying to fit onto the wood
like she's trying to fit into my ducts,
going for those tears.

My mom bought me fruit punch
from the pretzel vendor
on the way here after school.
I drink it and pull another card.

You'd think I was this rebel:
third grade poker player
in a therapist's office,
bullshitting through the hour.
The session ends and I collect
my bottle caps, walk home with my mother.

Get under the covers,
grab my kitten towards me.
Rock back and forth and weep.

ODE TO PEARLS

In a museum,
outside the gift shop,
in the bathroom,
my mother offers me
pearl earrings from Tiffany's.

Once when I was young,
we were broke,
groceries were a chore,
my grandmother gifted these
earrings to my mother
instead of milk.

These earrings
of rage, anger,
being handed to me;
an heirloom
in a public bathroom.

The posts rip through
my nearly closed holes.
I give a drop of blood.

I want you to have this pain.
I want you to take this pain from me.
Remember that I love you.
Remember how my mother loved me?
$400 Tiffany earrings
instead of a loaf of bread?

I'll buy you lunch,
you can take the train home.
Put these earrings in a drawer somewhere.
Take them from me.
Less reminder of a mother
who'd rather see me starve
than unadorned.

ODE TO CHICKENS

To cuddle with a chicken, first
find a comfortable chair
in your aunt and uncle's
Costa Rican kitchen.

Make sure you've finished
your fresh grapefruit juice
and fed the chickens
their lunch of corn kernels.

Sit down.
Wait for her
to be handed to you.
Grab her ankles
and pull her close.
Wrap your other arm around her.

If she's tired from eating,
running the farm,
and you're lucky,
she might fall asleep
against your twelve-year-old
cuddles.

Manhattan,
school,
all the fights back there,
the cars,
erased
in two little yellow
closed eyes.

I bet you thought
only kittens
slowed a heartbeat.

ODE TO PAPER PAJAMAS

I sit on the bed and the nurse
asks me if I know what manic depression is.
Do you know about your brain?
Did they explain in the emergency room?
Have they drawn you the diagram?

Someone in the hallway is yelling.
Someone in the quiet room is
sinking into a stupor.
Someone is being discharged.
The door to the outside
briefly unlocked.

Concentrate, Nina.
Do you know why you're here?

Somewhere my seventh grade classmates
wonder where I am.
Two weeks left of school,
probably out on the quad,
at the ice cream truck.

Here, I'll draw you a diagram.

I hear the shower in the next room turn on.
Someone is washing off the stale air,
using one-ounce shampoo,
putting on paper pajamas.

Nina, look at the paper.
Here is your brain:
up, and down, up and down.
Do you understand?
Do you understand why you're here?

Somewhere my mother is buying me
a container of strawberries.
Somewhere my sister
is crying in a school bathroom.

In a room in a psych ward
a twelve-year-old's brain
is scribbled on a pad.

Up and down.
Up and down.

ODE TO NOTIFICATIONS

There is a battle with the lover
before this one on the internet.

First my smile, brushed hair and dimples.
The sun behind us. Kiss on my cheek,
new love not looking at the camera.

His profile picture has two lovers eating BBQ.
Matching sunglasses.

It must have been from July Fourth,
he gushes, now that it's December.
I have always loved this picture.

He has eleven likes a picture, I have fifty.
I close my eyes and pretend
he is counting every single one.

Six months of love-posts are unearthed beneath his name.
They have all the same interests.

Love is about finding someone to be weird with.

I predetermine all my posts are public.
My lover is the best cook, their love is not about sex.

My lover buys me the best presents,
their love is real because they don't have to change.

My lover makes me laugh,
he posts a picture of them laughing.

I change my profile picture weekly,
wait a day to check his page.

Wonder if he'll accidentally friend request me
while stalking me,

swipe the screen on the left so
I don't make that same mistake.

He never had that pulsing glow behind his eyes with me.

I send telepathic messages through the internet:

I didn't either. This is not a loss.
I am happier now. I don't miss you.

Stare right at the camera,
right through the zoom lens at his face.

I swear we make eye contact
right before I click to share.

ODE TO SHRINKAGE

Sometimes I wonder
where the weight goes,
if you urinate it out,
sweat it out,
bloated out of your skin
onto the bed sheets.
Walk ten miles,
pee out a pound.
Every time I get smaller,
shrinking into the clothes in the attic
with my disappearing cycle
you can watch,
the pounds seep out my skin
while I sleep, walk,
talk to the guys.
You can see the difference
in how they look at me
with every bathroom break I take.
A puddle left on the floor
of invisibility;
a cloak of shed calories.
A figure wrung out,
left out on the line,
shrunk in the dryer,
everyone crowding around
to feel my new skin,
warm and dry.

ODE TO BONES

i want to be
a mess of bones
wrist bone
vertebrae
ankle nub
clavicle
you see if
i reach to the ceiling
there is a rib cage
the doctors
tell me i don't need
to lose more
but the bones
they're smooth
and flawless
what am i
if i don't show them off
a little?
we hunt elephants
for their tusks
lust for their ivory
don't care that
they die after
smooth bones
elegant bones
priceless bones
don't you want
to see my bones?
give me a glass
of ice water
and a salad
and maybe

we can look at them
together

ODE TO MY EMAIL DRAFT FOLDER

Oh draft folder,
graveyard of impulse control
where unsent love letters
take root,
angry rants left
to fester in privacy.
I've told off
friends,
ex-boyfriends,
hit cancel,
agreed to save.
I've dug plots for bullies,
won all the fights,
wooed all my crushes.
Forty drafts unfinished.
Forty wars.
Folder filled
with social victories,
while my sent emails
bail with apologies,
fold in confrontation.
Inbox ridden
with everyone else winning
the battles.
My draft folder
is the toughest girl I know.
Bows to no one,
out in the cloud,
a goddess no one has ever met,
wanting to swoop down,
but terrified she
can't stick the landing.

ODE TO THE GO GIRL, (OR ODE TO THE FUNNEL THAT LETS YOU PEE STANDING UP)

Go Girl you can pee
on a rock now.
Side of a building.
A urinal.
Walk the ten mile trail
with no porta potties
like a man.
Every tree potential target.
The dirt, a bull's eye.
Cup yourself,
Go Girl.
Write your name
on the pavement.
No more squatting.
No more mooning the houses
on the side.
Like a man.
Like the men you
pass on the trail
alone that make your stomach
a habitat to moths,
fluttering.
Go Girl on the side of the tree,
but watch the distance.
Keep your pants close.
Stay by the call box
Go Girl.
Keep it quiet.
Keep it sacred.
Put it back fast.
Your rubber
can't tackle
flesh.

ODE TO MEATBALLS

There are so many
ways to cook meatballs,
but in that first year
of the relationship
we would take the train home
from New York,
get out at the gas station,
my love, drunk on romance,
me, high from the
street lights of Manhattan.
I'd stumble, buy
a meatball sub,
sitting in the fridge
for God knows how long,
grey and soggy as
socks after a run in the rain.
I'd pay and
cram it in minutes:
grade D meat,
days old bread,
but so smitten
I swore it was gourmet.
You can take me
to the best restaurant
in Italy,
the meatballs
will never match
this sandwich:
the delicacy
of falling in love
on Tuesdays at midnight
in a Sonoco
on the side of the road.

ODE TO THE FIRE EXTINGUISHER

My brain has caught fire
a few minutes before I get on the bus.
Forty minutes later in a session it burns.

I can't put it out.
The fire extinguisher
in my apartment isn't working.

But you have an apartment.
You have love.
The fire is not keeping you
from the pillow.

The chair is burning through the floor.
I feel the floorboards
begin to weaken underneath.

Do you have a hose, I ask him.
I paid the receptionist.
We charged my insurance.
Is there a bucket of powder
to throw over the flames?

I think you're fine he tells me,
the hose sitting next to his chair.
You went to work today.
Your husband is in the waiting room.
Your cats are fed.

The door has caught fire.
My brains spill out onto the carpet.
I am melting.

Please. Help me put out the fire.
Tell me how to calm this.
Our session is over.
The office is in ashes.

Go home to your husband.
Go home to your cats.
Think of all the people worse off than you.
Think of all the people I need to help.

I fall through the floor.

We drive home.
My brain leaks into the bed sheets.
I wonder how long I can keep
scooping it back into my head.

ODE TO PUBLIC SERVANTS

You stand,
not too tall,
red faced under pressure.

Keep your lid on!
they tell you.
The pressure builds.

Someone screams!
You call to attention.
Saving lives like
it's no big deal.

And, although
it's your accomplices
who get the credit,

we all know
who really did the work.

Oh,
fire hydrant.

ODE TO PUBLIC TRANSIT

I don't know which is the gas
pedal and which are the brakes,
the emergency brake,
what a stick shift is.
Up here in the countryside
(which is anything north of Manhattan
for you country dwellers, up past the
Harlem 125th street station,
or Yonkers)
you have to drive
lest you be trapped
in your house
but I do not.
Once when I was ten
I ran in front of traffic,
at eleven I climbed the roof
of a school building,
seventeen it was the GW bridge,
eighteen it was a pair of nail clippers,
twenty-six it was a bottle of sleeping pills.
And you might see a car,
but I see a razor blade
or a knife
or a gun
and opt to get trapped
at work in a rainstorm
rather than have access
to death like that.

ODE TO PUBLIC ASSISTANCE

I still have my old food stamps card,
reduced fare MetroCard,
all the SSI letters asking how much I earn,
piles of old pay stubs,
even the letter when I graduated
to a full time job, full time bank account,
employee health insurance.

They think I was always one of them,
praise my work ethic despite the disability.

On the register is a girl who asks
them to cut her hours back
so she doesn't lose Medicaid.

In the deli is a girl
trying to figure out
how much is on her food stamps.

In the bottle room
is the guy who has to dig through
the garbage for nickels.

I left that shell
of living behind seven years ago
so they think I'm safe,
tell me how people would rather
live off the government than earn a paycheck.

I'm a wet dream for the people who believe
in boot straps.
The fantasy, the one who got off.

Meanwhile there's a trail
of money and benefits, stamps,
a rope attached to the top of a cliff
funded by tens of thousands
of dollars tied together,
that I climbed for thirteen years
before I got here.

ODE TO EARBUDS

My husband has named
all the walkers
in the neighborhood,
assuming they reside
in one of the "homes" here,
the types of places
I have lived.

The "Sidewalk Inspector"
who is bent against his will,
the "Rastafarian" who argues
with the cashier at Dunkin' Donuts,
the "Fancy Man" who walks with such an air
you'd think he was royalty.

These days, on my day off
or in the afternoon
I put my headphones in,
walk all over,
talking to myself sometimes,
sometimes actually on the phone.

We joke, *what have people named me?*
"The girl escaped from the mental ward,"
"The Arguer," "The Singer."

Be careful on your walks
they warn me,
so many characters to be worried about.

Meanwhile I rant and rave into my ear buds,
sometimes breaking into a sprint
to make the light, up and down the hills.

The unnamed walker, one of the crazies,
no longer in the institution,
making her way back home.

ODE TO METAPHORS

On the couch he murmurs
You and I are the imperfect socks at the dollar store.

Stoned he tells me
I saved all the other men you might pursue.

Over the hum of the ac he whispers
You're alright I guess.

After my haircut he states
Now you look presentable.

As I undress for him he mutters
You're a lump of pizza dough,
(but I'm your pepperonis.)

Once a man told me all the niceties
then evaporated into distant fog.

Once a man called me perfect,
then crossed the country, never turned around.

Whose soft arms hold me when I dream nightmares?
Whose hands cook my favorite meals?

Whose feet pound the gas pedal
because I fear a steering wheel?

Which would you rather?
Mismatched socks in the dollar store,

a book of rehearsed nothings
left on the desk for barren memories.

ODE TO QUARANTINE

Day one and there you are
with all the bottles of water,
ice that he brought you.
An adventure. A campout.
Pullout couch on the old sheets,
a couple of cats.

Day two and you start to think
about his pre-existing condition, his weaknesses,
but he's negative.

Day three and the cats
lay on you like they know
you have what's plagued
your anxiety for two years.
It's just a runny nose you tell them
no big deal.

Day four and you're having
nightmares about dying,
going to hell
as though you've committed murder
with your breath.

Google says you're
contagious for ten days.
It's been five.
You haven't left the cesspool.

Imagine your nose runs
but your husband could die.
Imagine post nasal
drip for two days
could leave you a widow.

Imagine your world
sitting on the couch,
the kind of love,
when they know you could kill them
in one breath,
keep you full of ice in the cooler,
bring you Tylenol,

keep you alive.

ODE TO THE PRESCRIPTION PAD

I am not going to raise your meds today.
You can calm down,
you're not listening.
You're pulsating,
your brain is touching the window.

I won't let you raise my meds today.

I told you I'm not raising your meds today.
Your illness is showing,
it must be showing all the time.

The chair is bigger than I am.
His bulging eyes
and prescription pad
a mallet
waiting to knock me out.

You're not changing my meds today.

I told you I'm not changing them.
What if you take a little more in the morning?
What if you lose your job?
What if your marriage crumbles?

You're not changing my meds today.

I told you I'm not changing them.
I could silence you,
so you could relax.
Aren't you exhausted?
Doesn't your brain
long to sit still?

You're not changing my meds today.

His grip tightens
on the pen used
to suck someone's personality
out through their nose.

I'll keep it the same for now,
think it over.
Accept your brain,
shrink it.
Come back next month.

Learn to
go to sleep
like the good girl I know you are.

ODE TO ANXIETY DISORDER

The day I panicked he was dead,
the beginning of the winter spiral,
I left work early to walk home to him,
practicing my speech
to the ambulance.
I was at work,
for the heart attack,
the suicide.
He had used my treadmill,
fell in the basement.
I didn't know he was dying,
I am always the one on the brink of that.
Ten minutes along the sidewalk:
would he be pronounced dead
on the basement floor?
In the living room?
At the hospital?
Crossing the street
with my phone in my hand,
911 on my fingertips.
In front of the house
my husband was taking out the trash.
Healthy arms lifting
garbage bags into the
dumpster.
We walked through the door together,
my brain unraveled,
his strong arm around my shoulder,

unphased.

ODE TO CAFFEINE

My best friend Andrew
did coke because it feels like mania
if you've ever felt mania.
When I drink enough coffee
it's not the same
but it's almost the same.
He graduated to crack,
I spent the summer
getting high on energy drinks
while they pumped me full of sedatives
to get me to fall asleep at night.
Andrew died because he couldn't
kick his crack addiction.
I cried for days.
Took medicine to numb it
drank coffee to stay awake.
It's just coffee until
you're at the emergency room for
your heart pounding in your ears
while your friend is gone,
memory in a graveyard.
You sneak to Starbucks
to wake up,
drink until your eyes are throbbing.
A bottle of sedatives
in your purse,
just in case,
always ready.

ODE TO BEAN

On the days my friends die,
which has never been
a rare occurrence,
I learn the news
and it drips off of me,
my skin waterproof
to the dead.

Drugs,
suicide,
accident,
murder,
drama,
hysteria,
meltdowns.

I'm fine.
I'm always fine.

When the cat was laying limp
in my hand,
a needle in her paw
after suffering quietly
for what weeks?
Months?
The vet closed her eyes
at my request,
holding a stethoscope to her fur
listening for the slowing
heartbeat:

slow, slow, stop.

She was still,
my pulse speeding up;
my heart beating out through me,
the room a whirlwind.

Cats don't tell you when it's time
out loud,
just purr loudly on the table
at the doctor's office.

Humankind
could never be so stoic.

ODE TO POLICIES

Manic depressives
are not life insurable,
the lithium in our purses
a liability.
The internet says:
Bipolar people live ten to
twenty years less
than the average person.
For policies,
sadness is too
high a payout risk.
Once a year at work
they come to offer us life insurance.
I don't sign up,
me and all the other bipolars
busy on line waiting to die
decades early.
Our loved ones left
with our med bottles,
our coffins.
The insurance providers
at their desks,
smugly thinking,

I told you so.

ODE TO BEING THICK SKINNED

When you're a child sometimes at a party,
they take a balloon and cover it with shaving cream,
hand you a razor.

Shave this balloon they tell you.
Don't let it pop.
Just take the shaving cream off.

Everyone thinks the girl is
the sweetest girl.

Here is our love. The shaving cream.
We will cover you from toenail to hair follicle.

Then. The razors.
Handed out to everyone in the building.

You're so kind, surely you won't notice
all of our blades.

You're so good. Look at how you handle
what so many others could not.

Look at how strong you are.
Look at how the razor just
pulls a little but you stay intact.

The children at the party all have their balloons
and giggle and smile and love and play.

But eventually the balloons all pop,
everyone has lost.

Eventually the sharp edge of the razor
hits the skin at just the right angle,
all the air comes flying out.

Nothing left but torn rubber
laying all over the yard.

ODE TO STARTING ANTI-ANXIETY MEDS

I'm an unclenched fist.
A post sneeze nose.
Your scalp when you get the knot out of your hair.
The moment your new shoes are broken in.
Also your shoes after you clip your toenails.
Your face after getting waxed.
Your legs under the blankets after shaving.
Your right nostril after you finally blow it during a cold.
Your lungs after you finish choking.
Your back after you get the itch.
Your face when you take your mask off.
When you finish peeing after holding it the whole car ride.
The glass of water after a run.
Your eyes opening after a bad dream.
The feeling of freedom after four months
of being so rigid your heart could barely keep a rhythm.

ODE TO BRAINS

Two pills, one pill, five pills,
three times a day
to fix the brain.
Breakfast lunch dinner
sleeping pills at night.
Are you embarrassed about your brain?
I open the pill box and offer it to everyone.
Some say
I already took mine.
Some say,
I probably need them.
Are you embarrassed about your brain?
If I told you that we are all crazy,
and to talk about it,
would you?
My head is cut open,
everyone can see
how it's busted.
They keep the bandages over theirs,
tell me in secret
they've had to sew theirs together
just as much as I have.
Two pills, one, five,
three times a day.
My pill box rattles
in my pocket.
They'll tell you to hide it
in the folds of your clothes,
but if you want to know,
we are all naked underneath.

EPILOGUE

Thoughts on faith
(reprise)

ODE TO SAINT DYMPHNA

Sometimes faith comes out of nowhere,
on a snowy day,
snowflakes touching
your face like a loved one,
landing in your hair
like soft fingertips
melting into and soothing you.
Maybe when the bees pollinate flowers,
or there are cacti with water in the desert,
coconuts in the jungle.
Or sometimes, maybe,
someone gifts you a laminated card
of the patron saint of mental disorders
even though you're Jewish.
You take her anyway,
carry her in your pocket
throughout your adventures
and work and life,
forget she's there
as you go about your day.
Then one day a woman
approaches you with a
brain as broken as yours,
worn out as you are,
recognizes your saint
peeking out of your shirt pocket,
admits she has the same devotion.
Suddenly even though you're strangers,
you're Jewish and mostly agnostic
and Saint Dymphna was a present
from someone you barely knew
your faith intertwines with a similar person.
Maybe God is real,
maybe God is not real

but we are real and here we are.
Trying to get through it.
With snowflakes or bees or church.
Or maybe a crumpled, laminated card
in our pockets of a woman
who knows we suffer,
or we imagine knows we suffer,
soothing us as we work
or shop at the grocery store,
busy, absentmindedly hoping for peace.

ACKNOWLEDGEMENTS

I would like to acknowledge John Smaldone, Lindsay Milne, Chris Vollaro, Lynne Volkmann, and Jennifer Martinez for helping me get through the worst bipolar episode I had in nearly a decade, which almost cost me my job and marriage, however also inspired half the poems in this book.

Without my art, my bipolar would do me in completely, and without my friends, I would never survive my symptoms.

"Ode to bacteria" was featured in *Painting Poetry and Music* in Peekskill, NY.

"Ode to chickens" first appeared in *Memory House Magazine*

"Ode to bones" was first featured in *Boned*

"Ode to the prescription pad" was first featured in *All the Sins*

PRAISE FOR *WARM BLOODED TREE*

Nina Belén Robins writes with gripping authenticity, creating poems that hall-mark the human condition. Any reader will relate to the various themes and circumstances illustrated by her words.
— *Cassandra Alfred, author of "This is How You Love Her"*

❖

To use a line from one of her poems, *"they've seen me at last,"* Warm Blooded Tree has a way of capturing the vulnerability and desperation in loneliness that many of us are led to believe is unique to only a select few.

In spite of that, so many of Robins' poems paint a poignant picture of the universal craving for connection we all experience, and how the small seemingly insignificant bright spots of contact help to connect us to the humanity and compassion we often take for granted. Her vulnerability and insight into the human condition is arresting, and after reading her most recent book, once again I feel like I have been caught in the embrace of her words.
— *Adam Biggs, NPS poet and artist from NY*

❖

Who among us has not known loneliness? Nina Belén Robins' poems in Warm Blooded Tree will creep into the empty spaces that haunt your soul at night and remind you just how human and vulnerable you are. Her adroit ability to weave you into her stories whether you think you belong there or not is as present in her newest book as it was in the three before it.

Get ready to experience some feelings with this powerful collection of perspicacious poetry. — *Danni Green poet and singer*

WARM BLOODED TREE

Nina Belén Robins

Loneliness. Scorn. Hope.

Emotions we've all felt.

In *Warm Blooded Tree*, Robins captures these primal feelings with uniquely vivid images, perfectly selected words and scenes that stay with the reader long after the poem's last line.

available online
in paperback and
ebook format

PRAISE FOR *T. GONDII*

Having had the pleasure of reading all three of this author's published books, it is no surprise that she continues to amaze and move me with her poetry. Her collection takes you on a journey, and draws you into her world, full of pain and love, and of course cats! She is an inspiration to me, and I cannot recommend this (and her other two books) highly enough!
— *Deb Klein*

❖

I loved reading this. I especially appreciated "To my Future Mother in Law" and "Consent." Not only is this well written, it makes me feel less alone. I love the raw honesty and total exposure on these pages. Nina perfectly captures so many of the things I've experienced. Reading this felt like sitting down with a friend who gets it. — *KH*

❖

"Buy the ticket, take the ride" This is an amazing collection of thoughts, struggles and stories of a truly amazing woman. This collection does not disappoint. — *Thanh Wisler*

T. GONDII
Nina Belén Robins

With searing honesty and ferocious wit, noted poet and mental health advocate Robins illuminates the brutal internal and external pressure to bear children; and the courage, self-awareness, love—and pain—required to remain child-free. Just when her words become near-unbearable, she throws in a sly and hilarious poem about cats.

available online
in paperback and
ebook format

PRAISE FOR *A BED WITH MY NAME ON IT*

Bookended by movingly hopeful poems, this collection carries the reader into places we may never have been and may hope never to go to. But having been there and come through—with the writer—with humor, deep humanity, and an energizing self-acceptance, we're better for it. These poems have the music of performance poetry in them and the power of crafted literary work. We have here a very satisfying and rare merger of talent, humility and valuable life experience. No poem fell flat for me. Every poem invites and rewards multiple readings. —*Elizabeth K. Gordon*

❖

If you have ever had a moment that made you feel out of control, this book has a poem for you. Several, in fact, and not one of them gives you a feeling of anything less than survival at its finest.Don't forget this poet's name. Nina will have a long career. You won't forget the poetry. —*Wil Gibson*

❖

I read this book in one sitting! Nina brought us into her life and spread light into so many places so often left in the dark. It was a pleasure to share her perspective. I work with girls in a community residence and I could relate to each page with the girls I have worked with as well as my own personal experiences. This was so powerful. —*Amanda*

❖

Nina's book *A Bed with my Name on It* is tragic beauty. The poems are filled with so much raw emotion, each one is like a gut punch of "damn." I'm very grateful for her poems. —*Nick Yuk*

A BED
WITH MY
NAME
ON IT

Nina Belén Robins

This book of poems draws on the
author's experience within the
mental health system from the
time she was a little girl until she
reached her early twenties. The
poems illuminate the soul-numb-
ing degradations that spurred her
to find her way out of the system
and the kindnesses that made it
possible.

available online
in paperback and
ebook format

PRAISE FOR *SUPERMARKET DIARIES*

This magnificent volume of poetry is the author's first published book but surely not her last. With impeccable insight and a vivacious appreciation for the human condition, Robins takes us on a journey behind the supermarket check-out counter. She offers us a unique glimpse into the lives of the ordinary people who cross her path each day, using her incredible poetic talents to convince us of the extra-ordinary humanity of each of them, and by extension, of ourselves. I highly recommend this book! — *choirqueer*

❖

Simple observations, expressed with great insight, wisdom and eloquence. — *Dan Couture*

❖

In a variety of stories through the eyes of a creatively observant cashier, Nina's writing is sharp witted, emotional, and promises to be very memorable! — *Zadra*

❖

This is *The Spoon River Anthology* of supermarkets: insightful poems about customers, staff and life behind the cash register, by an exciting young NYC poet. Can't wait for the next book! — *Lori Ubell*

SUPER-MARKET DIARIES

Nina Belén Robins

Mild-mannered grocery store employee by day, Nina Robins is a well-known performance poet who has twice performed at the National Poetry Slam. Her poetry has been described as "exceptionally appealing," "heartbreakingly honest," and "subversively deep for work so overtly entertaining."

—Taylor Mali, author of
What Teachers Make

available online
in paperback and
ebook format

Nina Belén Robins is a three-time National Slam Poet, and author of the books of poetry: *Supermarket Diaries, A Bed With My Name On It, T. Gondii.* and *Warm Blooded Tree.*

She spent much of her life in various institutions, but has finally broken free and lives with her husband and cats, working in the bakery department of a supermarket.

She writes whenever possible, and wants to help normalize and destigmatize mental illness as best she can.

CPSIA information can be obtained
at www.ICGtesting.com
Printed in the USA
JSHW080443150223
37715JS00003B/16